Cooking
for
Nitwits

Cooking for Nitwits

Rosemary Wells and Johanna Hurley

Photographs by Barbara Olcott

And featuring Lee Bryant

E. P. DUTTON / DIAL BOOKS

NEW YORK

Publisher's Note: This book is a spoof, a send-up of America's
passion for cookbooks and home entertaining.
The recipes and instructions contained in this book
are meant in jest and are not to be followed.
Any brand names that have been included in this book
have been used because they are popular brands.
Nothing derogatory is meant by their inclusion in this book.

Published in the United States by E. P. Dutton and Dial Books,
divisions of Penguin Books USA Inc.,
2 Park Avenue, New York, N.Y. 10016.

Published simultaneously in Canada
by Fitzhenry and Whiteside, Limited, Toronto.

Library of Congress Cataloging-in-Publication Data

Wells, Rosemary.
     Cooking for nitwits / Rosemary Wells and Johanna Hurley
   photographs by Barbara Olcott and featuring Lee Bryant. — 1st ed.
         p.   cm.
     ISBN 0-525-48503-1
     1. Cookery—Humor.   I. Hurley, Johanna.   II. Title.
   PN6231.C624W45   1989
   818'.5402—dc20   89-32255
                    CIP

10 9 8 7 6 5 4 3 2 1

First Edition

Cooking
for
Nitwits

Holiday Entertaining

Please Don't Eat the Place Card!
Gatorade Gelatin Mold

Using a laundry-type indelible ink pen, we personalize name tags for each of our guests.

Place to the left of each guest's table setting.

Here is a fresh idea to reduce place setting clutter- set your place cards in an edible thirst-quenching gelatin salad.

You will need...
Lemon-lime Gatorade
Several small decorative gelatin molds
"Hello... My Name Is..." stick-on labels

Dissolve gelatin in heated
Gatorade, and fill each
individual mold with mixture.
Then, as easy as one-two-three,
slip place cards, name-side down,
into the filled molds.
Chill until set. Serve on a
bed of crisp lettuce.

Alternate serving suggestion:

Arrange on a large platter
and let guests enjoy finding
their names and helping
themselves.

American Heritage Bean Sampler

Our rich Colonial heritage gives us this recipe. How many times have we seen a sampler framed on a wall and wished the colors and sentiments could appear on our very own Thanksgiving table?

Here's how ⌐

You will need...

A large baking dish
As many kinds of colorful beans
   as you can find in local stores
Wax paper
Bricks
Honey
Vinaigrette

Coat the bottom of the pan with honey. Honey never, ever dries. It will hold the beans in place while you create your design. One of the most popular proverbs is "God give me the strength to change what I can, etc...."

Getting started

The finished piece

Your heirloom salad should be started a week to ten days before Thanksgiving. We enjoy working on the sampler a bit each evening while watching TV or while chatting with a close friend.

After the beans are snugly arranged in the final pattern, cover them with wax paper. Gently place the bricks on top of the paper so that the beans cannot move around. Now fill the pan with water.

Place in a 350°F. oven for about four hours or until beans are tender.

The honey will dissolve in the first two minutes. But, add water as necessary.

You'll know when the sampler is done. Remove from oven, cool, then refrigerate.

After hours of careful and detailed work, our beautiful sampler is ready to serve—not only a feast for the eyes, but for the palate, too.

Drizzle with vinaigrette dressing and scoop up a hearty portion for each guest.

Add water

"Beat-the-Clock" Galantine

A galantine of any fowl is one of the most festive and splendid dishes in our repertoire and can be served for any holiday. It calls for removing all bones from the bird while retaining its exact shape in the final assembly. Standard recipes take days to complete, but we've discovered a short-cut method anyone can do in fifteen minutes.

Place a raw 20-pound turkey on a table in front of you.

Start anywhere⏤

Cut the meat from the left drumstick, for example. (Make a note whether "left" means your left or the bird's left.)

Saving time requires good organizational skills. Therefore, fill out inexpensive labels for all major parts of the turkey. Attach appropriate tag (in this case "left drumstick") to the meat which has just been removed and set it aside in a logical scheme.

Careful identification of fowl parts and accurate tagging pay off when you begin the reassembly stage.

Proceed until all meat is removed from the carcass, safely labeled and arranged.

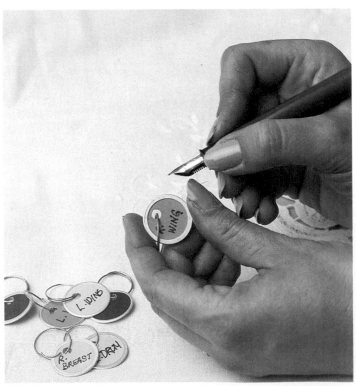

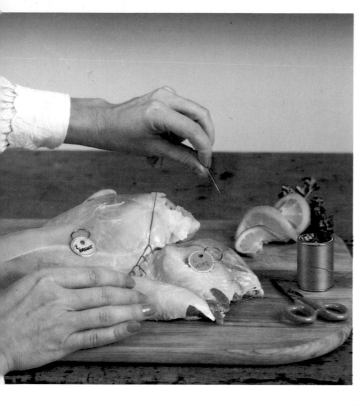

Now using light colored thread, re-create the turkey perfectly by sewing it neatly together, much as you would the back, front, and sleeves of a tiny sweater.

When the turkey is completely reassembled, roll it gently into a compact shape. Place in a large crock and cover with your favorite cooking wine.

Place a heavy weight on top.

The turkey will quickly marinade while you make the stuffing.

Free-standing stuffing

Kitchen Wisdom: A little-known scientific fact about stuffing

Even the cheapest store-bought stuffing has limitless possibilities for form and shape. When combined in proper proportions with liquid, exposed to warm air, and left alone in a dark, quiet room for an hour or so, your stuffing will rise like the finest yeast bread!

Remove it at once from the mixing bowl before it "falls back." Then, see how easy it is to mold into the shape of a turkey.

Taking on the shape of the turkey

Remove rolled turkey
from crock.

Place stuffing form
inside.

Roast in a 350°F. oven
until tender and
golden brown.

The Galantine — presented with pride
on your holiday table.

✚ Safety First Reminder ✚

When cleaning up after any raw poultry, attention must be paid to possible salmonella contamination.

The most sensible way to tackle salmonella is head-on with antibiotics. Nobody honestly finishes all ten days of any penicillin or tetracycline prescription. The extra six or seven capsules usually sit in our medicine cabinets for months or even years. Put these valuable germ killers to good use instead.

Liberally sprinkle the cutting board, your hands, and all utensils with the powders and pellets from these multicolored wonder drugs, and feel assured you've protected your family wisely.

Sweet Potato Snow Drift

Did you ever wonder how the math that you studied in grade school would ever be of use to you again? This Thanksgiving gather the children around you as you create this dish, and they will delight in seeing applied math right in their own home.

An intimate knowledge of weights and counter balances is the foundation of this recipe. The sweet potatoes are whipped light and airy and placed in the serving dish. Our rich homemade marshmallows are made with egg whites and rich double cream and are filled with old-fashioned nougat. Each weighs four ounces and therein lies a secret from the discipline of simple physics.

Although the effect is rather spontaneous, solid principles of geometry give this dish its stability. See diagram which illustrates the side-angle-side theorem at work in our recipe.

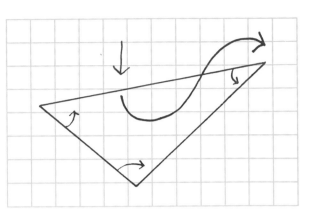

For maximum drift, scatter marshmallows on top of the sweet potatoes. You will find that the weight of the marshmallows, acting like an inverted fulcrum, allows the potatoes to whirl up, around, and sometimes over the dish.

O Tannenbaum Blinking Torte

Here is a radiant dessert from Bavaria, the cradle of Christmas.

Fill your favorite pastry shell with mincemeat or any other traditional holiday filling. Throw in a string of decorative lights at the last minute, cover with pastry and bake in a 350°F. oven until golden.

Lower the lights in your dining room just before entering with this spectacular torte.

Easter Island Sorbet Heads

The world of the archeologist inspires this dessert. Huge stone statues, carved hundreds of years ago, loom on Easter Island's landscape, deep in the heart of Polynesia. Some of these statues rise as high as forty feet. They stare mysteriously out to sea. No one yet knows who carved these immense figures or why.

You will need...

Raspberry, lemon, and lime sorbet
Easter grass

Remove sorbet from freezer. Scoop and form rough shape on nest of Easter grass. Carve fine features.

Gloves may hamper your sculpting skills; however, you will need to work in a cold kitchen. Open the windows and lower the temperature to 30° F. or less.

Each time we release a figure from the sorbet we inch a little closer to the Truth.

"Lite" Cooking

There is absolutely no need to sacrifice rich sauces and luscious desserts while losing pounds. Any good nutritionist will tell you that the keys to successful weight loss are eating a balanced diet and controlling the amount of food you eat.

217 Calorie Five Course Dinner

Appetizer
½ inch slice of avocado on leaf of Boston lettuce (14 calories)

Soup
1 teaspoon vichyssoise (22 calories)

Fish Course
1 batter-dipped deep-fried bay shrimp
with smidgeon of Dijon mustard sauce (18 calories)

Entree
Miniature Beef Wellington with dot of Bernaise sauce (53 calories)
⅛ baked potato with dab of butter and sour cream (26 calories)
Asparagus tips with dash of Hollandaise sauce (12 calories)

Dessert
Sliver of nine-layer triple chocolate cake (72 calories)

Sample dinner: only 217 calories, considerably less than the average weight-watching frozen entree!

Caves du Barque

On a recent tour of the French wine country, we encountered Pierre and Marie, gardener and cook on the Vichy estate in Provence. We convinced them to reveal a rare scientific miracle to us.

Pierre is the only living veteran of the Franco-Prussian War. Marie tells us her mother was Napoleon's personal maid. No one knows for sure, but conservative estimates put their birthdates around 1856 to 1859.

The secret of their longevity can be found in the bark of the Broulliard trees. Once these mighty trees proliferated, but now only three or four Parcs Broulliard remain in Europe.

We were led to the Vichy wine cellars and their "Cave du Barque." There in the cool depths of stone, centuries old and hidden, is one of the few "Caves du Barque" left in France today.

Pierre places the Broulliard bark in the finest cognac. Marie adds blueberries from her jardin du cuisine for flavor. The mixture is then carefully fermented for thirty days in the "cave."

When the bark is ready, it is dried, then crumbled and sprinkled like cinnamon on buttered toast.

Once in the bloodstream, this all natural mega-fiber power-packed cholesterol buster attacks fat cells, neutralizing them permanently.

This miraculous fat-destroyer acts much like a detergent in the blood, emulsifying and pulverizing the harmful LDLs while leaving the healthful HDLs completely alone.

Vive Pierre and Marie!

Tight Cooking: Budget Specials

A dilemma for today's young marrieds is wishing to entertain on the same grand scale as their Mom and Dad. No need to call Mom for an extra $300 till the end of the month— we've provided this fine collection of recipes, inspired by dinners served at the poshest Park Avenue parties. These dishes have been slightly revised and are offered here at a fraction of their original cost.

Faux Saumon Mousse on Bed of Tapioca Caviar

You will need...
   Ink from one female squid
   2 cups prepared fine pearl tapioca

Ask your fishmonger to make sure that the squid you buy is a female. He will know by the tell-tale five point star pattern that distinguishes the male from the female of the species.

In order to get the squid to release its ink, it is necessary to alarm it first. Begin by bringing the squid into a darkened room and holding it over the bowl of tapioca. Since red is the only color that squids can see, you must hold a flashing red light 10 to 12 inches from the squid.

Yell loudly!

The moment it senses the danger, the squid will release quantities of the black ink. Mix with the tapioca~for a "caviar" so rich it could fool the czar!

·~ᴑᵔᵔᴑ~·

"Caviar comes from a virgin sturgeon
A virgin sturgeon is a very rare fish
Not many sturgeons like to be virgins
That's why caviar is a very rare dish."

Alfred Lord Tennyson 1809-1892

·~ᴑᵔᵔᴑ~·

If you treat your squid kindly, it will supply you with ink for life. The Cape Cod chapter of the ASPCA recommends that you not "ink" your squid more than once a month.

Faux Saumon Mousse

You will need...

3 pounds Spam or your favorite canned luncheon loaf
1 tube anchovy paste
1 quart clam broth

Marinate the luncheon loaf in clam broth overnight. Remove to food processor and puree with anchovy paste. Place into an oiled copper fish mold and chill until firm.

Faux saumon mousse on bed of tapioca caviar. Savings: $120

✚ Good Health Alert: A word to the wise about botulism ✚

When using any canned food in recipes, we should all be wary of the botulism bacteria that can contaminate these tinned goods. Most of the time, when bacteria gets a good grip on the can it puffs out the top or the bottom of the metal and you can almost see for yourself the dangers inside.

However, to be on the safe side, we place our can opener near the bird's cage.

Everyone knows that canaries are used in the mines to detect lethal gasses, and so they are in the kitchen.

1. Open all cans near your bird's cage.

2. Watch his behavior for a few minutes before you eat anything from the can.

3. If he looks a little wobbly, discard the can immediately.

Phake Pheasant Under Glass

No need to befriend a gun-toting gamesman in order to serve your guests pheasant. Here is a step-by-step method for taking a common chicken and transforming it into the British gentry's favorite fowl.

You will need...
One large chicken, muslin wraps, sticks, leaves, pine needles, peppercorns, and a hammer

The first step in making a pheasant is to shrink the chicken. This is easily achieved by putting the chicken into a dryer on the hottest setting for two hours. Like a good woolen sweater, it will become several sizes smaller. As the bird tumbles, it should sound like a pair of sneakers drying.

Place in dryer.   Tumble dry for 2 hours. Remove

Remove the chicken from the dryer and wrap in layers of sticks, leaves, and pine needles, then tightly bind in muslin and compress in your trash compactor. This will cause the bird to develop a slightly "gamey" flavor.

Check for adequate shrinkage

Into the trash compactor!

Muslin wrap

Randomly hammer peppercorns into the meat to give the effect of "shot."

Now, like many a wiley restaurateur, you no longer have an ordinary chicken, but a pheasant!

Serve garni under a glass bell. Savings: $40

Puttin' on the Ritz

You will need...
   1 box Ritz crackers
   beef bouillon
   Red food coloring
   Steak sauce
   Boiled Thunderbird wine.

Soak the crackers in bouillon and red food coloring (3 drops medium rare, 5 drops rare). Carefully shape into individual filet mignons. Coat with steak sauce and move onto the barbecue grill. Turn once after 15 minutes and serve with wine sauce.

Filet Mignon, rare, with Madiera sauce. (No one will know that the beef is Ritz crackers and the sauce is pure Thunderbird.) Savings: $27

Highway Dividers— Gardens of Earthly Delights

Little known to the general public is the wealth of wild vegetables that grows so abundantly along many of America's highways and byways. Birds drop these seeds on their flight south in autumn. By the next summer, a tangle of treasures has grown to maturity. Without spending a penny, we have found luscious salads hidden in the copses and leas of our local parkways.

There— just under the tall grass!

All these "treasure-finds" are grown without harmful insecticides or fertilizers, and so enhance our dinner table naturally!

Wild Bibb!

Wild endive mixes with
the phlox and goldenrod.
Wild lettuces range from
Bibb to Boston and
nestle unencumbered
beneath the clover and
Queen Anne's lace.

Wild mushrooms,
    wild tomatoes,

the list is endless in
Mother Nature's garden.

Wild endive!

This "basket of plenty" was harvested in less than one hour of delightful hunt alongside a well-known parkway. We can't tell you exactly where, of course, but you'll enjoy discovering your very own secret roadside garden!

Highway harvest   Savings: $33

⚮ Just What the Doctor Ordered ⚮

Doctors prescribe capsules, tonics, and syrups left and right, but give us no advice on how to coerce patients into taking these unpalatable prescriptions. Nurses, however, know that a happy patient will recover with three times the speed of an unhappy patient. We have received hundreds of unsolicited tips from nurses across the country. Here we offer the best of the nurses' ideas that will tempt the palate of our under-the-weather friends.

Perking up the patient

Floating Vitamin Island
—tempting and healthful

It's just no fun to be sick. We are always looking for games. good books, and other distractions for the patient. Here is a "brilliant" idea which will surprise and delight our bored sick patient.

Flaming Robitussin Jubilee

Robitussin Jubilee

Start with a scoop of vanilla ice cream, pour syrup over cherries, and flambé.

Sominex Chocolate Bunnies

For the insomniac — healers in the ancient Greek and Roman empires knew of the sleep-inducing qualities of chocolate. These adorable bunnies, with the added ingredient of Sominex, will give you or your patient a night of healing slumber.

Sweet dreams!

The Get-Well-icles

Instead of mixing fruit with your patient's yogurt, mix in whatever the doctor has ordered and freeze overnight for a delicious and soothing treat that will keep those alimentary flora from running out on you.

The Get-Well-icles
For whatever ails you — counterclockwise from top — Cod Liversicle, Donnagelicle, Pepto Bismicle, Tetracyclicle, Eucalypticle, Asperinicle. All served with Erythromycin dip.

Warning: As with all over-the-counter medication, do not take Robitussin, Sominex, vitamins, or antibiotics without reading the label carefully or consulting your physician.

Homemade Bouillon Cubes

For those patients who just can't eat, we want to provide the maximum nourishment in the minimum volume.

Who knows what goes into mass-produced, dried soup stocks? We don't even want to tell you! This recipe requires a stock simmered for 24 hours and made from 10 chickens and 20 pounds of good green and yellow vegetables.

Any good kitchen equipment store can furnish you with a bouillon cuber. They are a bit pricey, but after a thousand cubes they pay for themselves.

Start the cuber when the stock has been reduced from 30 quarts to about ½ cup of rich, delicious "sludge."

The sludge is poured into the top of the cuber, which extracts the essential vitamins and nutrients from the last of the liquid and produces several power packed cubes, where you know every ingredient.

Remember:
    You can always tell a fake...

a homemade bouillon cube bounces.

New Frontiers in Pharmacological Pastry

28-Day Birth Control Cheesecake

Never forget a pill again with the 28-Day Birth Control Cheesecake! Developed by an eminent obstetrician, Dr. Mildred Steinway Barker, of Cedars of Lebanon Memorial Medical Center, Humana, Illinois, this treat is so tantalizing that you must make sure you don't eat more than one slice per day.

Dr. Mildred Steinway Barker

What's Hot, What's Not

Our trend spotters have found the words "blackened" and "creole" popping up on menus all over the country. While New Orleans cooking is all the rage with the arriviste yuppie set, the authentic genius of Cajun cuisine has barely surfaced.

"Blackening" food is a tradition as old as the Mississippi Delta. Henri, our favorite creole cook from the heart of the bayou, tells us that no self-respecting Cajun would eat anything that <u>wasn't</u> blackened.

Here we have blackened an entire meal, as found in the homes and native bistros of New Orleans. From bread and butter, gumbo, beer, and pie — all have been authentically blackened.

.·°C·°°·~°.

Blackened Chicken Gumbo

Blackened Creole Bread
with Blackened Butter
Blackened Crayfish Andouille
Blackened Crab Boil Okra
Blackened Red Potatoes and Corn
Blackened Beans and Rice.

Blackened Beer

Blackened Ponchatoula Pecan Pie
.·°C~·°·C~°.

Primal Scream Meatballs

Hundreds of self-help fads have sprouted like dandelions in the nuttiest of our fifty states, California, but the only fad that has really lasted is Classic Primal Scream Therapy.

But why go to the expense of reenacting your own birth, or re-creating in a giant scale your childhood nursery, when it's so easy to go back to that important moment with this recipe.

Primal Scream Meatballs
in Devil's Tongue Lava Sauce

Start with hot Mexican sausage. Add cayenne
pepper, Tabasco sauce, and Szechuan peppers.

Simmer for ten minutes in "King of Siam"
Devil's Tongue Lava Sauce (in the famous
bright yellow tin, available on any Thai
grocery supply mailing list).

Serve on a bed of jalapeños.

Peanut Butter and Jelly Sushi

For ten years sushi bars have dominated the New York and San Francisco restaurant scene. Sushi may be popular, but we've heard that some of our big-city pace setters secretly hate slimy raw fish, but won't admit it publicly.

Step 1:
Spread rice on seaweed wrapper

Step 2:
Apply peanut butter and jelly

Step 3:
Roll and cut sushi

Keeping the rare nutrients found in the seaweed wrapper, we have substituted for the fish that delicious American staple—peanut butter and jelly—and come up with a dish to delight the palates of both East and West!

...⚬ Time Savers and Helpful Hints ⚬...

Dishwasher Dinner Deluxe

Can today's women have high-powered careers and happy husbands as well? You bet! Women are now free to compete in the job market without sacrificing one bit of quality in the kitchen. Here is an executive secret direct from the corporate boardroom.

Who would have ever guessed that the working gal's best friend would be her dishwasher?

..⚬⚬⚬⚬..
Escarole Jimbale

Veal Oscar
Braised Celery
Scalloped Potatoes

Crème Brulee

Hot Mulled Cider
..⚬⚬⚬⚬..

Off to work and right
on time!

This time saver is prepared
in the morning before work.
Wrap each dish securely
in several layers of
aluminum foil. Place
in the dishwasher with
your breakfast dishes.
Let the "heavy-duty
pots and pans" cycle run.

Sweep him off his feet
with this evening feast.
He'll never understand
how you do it all!

A romantic dinner by
candlelight on
clean, warm china

Sunday Evening Leftover Sphinx

All of us who remember Sunday night suppers at our grandmothers' houses will recall when cook made the deliciously decadent puree of all the leftovers she had saved from midday dinner into what she called a "sphinx." We'd get to eat in the spacious kitchen for one thing, a great treat! And we'd be a little lax in our table manners for the only time during the week. What joy!

If cook was artistically inclined, she'd put in onion eyes and a lettuce hood or mane. If not, it was just plain, but plainly divine, too.

Take any leftovers you don't wish to give to the dogs. Combine and puree. (A trip to your antique dealer will easily provide you with an old sphinx mold.)

Grease inside of mold. Pour puree into mold. Bake for one hour and turn out onto an attractive platter.

Here from a gentler, quieter prewar era is a Sunday evening Sphinx.

"What's for lunch, Mom?"

Food Rockets!

Your children will look forward to lunchtime if they know they'll find a few food rockets tucked in with the hard-boiled eggs and Thermos of milk. Here's an action-packed snack that the lunchroom aides may not appreciate, but your child will thank you for. Better than any note that says "I love you," these food rockets will thrill and delight even the most recalcitrant child.

Serving suggestion: Food rockets with cubed Swiss cheese and Genoa salami

☞ Legal only in some states.

Talking to Your Food

The science pages of <u>The New York Times</u> as well as <u>Scientific American</u> and <u>American Botanist</u> inform us that conversation with house plants helps produce glossy leaves and abundant flowers.

Likewise, cheerful coaxing of a less than perky chicken or a bluefish with the blahs may be the critical difference between a one-star meal and a five-star meal.

Don't be embarrassed. When you're alone in the kitchen, murmur an encouraging word to that sad salad and be assured that the top chefs in the Michelin Guide became supreme in their field because of friendly conversations with all the ingredients in their dishes.

Our Favorite Desserts

Touch of Mink Parfait

The last time this spectacular dessert was seen was just before the Depression in 1929. Many a family included these mink-rimmed parfait glasses in a beloved daughter's trousseau. Now, we see them reappearing at estate sales all over the country, still in remarkably good condition.

Here is an elegant chocolate layered parfait served as they did at the most sought after turn-of-the-century dinner parties.

Use your best manners and hand wash only.

Stormy Weather Soufflé

Soufflés are notorious for collapsing at the drop of a hat. Not ours! Our grand Marnier soufflé has all the delicacy and flavor found on the finest French tables, but is durable enough to stand up to the test of turbulence....

Our secret: Tucked into the rich soufflé mixture is a sturdy balloon.

Bake soufflé gently and when fully risen, remove from the oven.

Stamp sharply on the floor, causing the soufflé to fall naturally. Then, reinflate by blowing on the mouthpiece of the balloon.

Kitchen Wisdom: Make sure you use the best eggs!

Pay a visit to your local egg farm. Tell the egg farmer you insist on eggs from only the chickens at the top of the pecking order. He will be surprised at your savvy.

Little known to the general public, these distinctive eggs with their luminous whites and marigold yolks have virtually no cholesterol and twice the protein of ordinary eggs. These are the eggs that find their way to the President's breakfast table.

These eggs can now be ordered from the Royal New England Egg Farms at less than $50 a dozen, just by dialing 1-800-Egg-Yolk.

You can walk through the storm
with your head held high knowing
that neither rain nor snow nor
dark of night shall cause this
soufflé to fall.

Cookies 'n' Clams

Let's throw out some of our old notions about what goes with what, and surprise our guests with a wild new dessert combo— cookies and clams.

The best of two tasty worlds. Our raw bar gives us cherrystones, cold and fresh as the morning's ocean catch, poised delicately atop our hot-out-of-the-oven whole-wheat chocolate chip cookie.

Delightfully new 'n' delicious too.

✚ Health Alert: A word about shellfish ptomaine ✚

Decades ago every school child in the state of Maine knew this little rhyme. It is a foolproof way to tell a good clam from a bad one.

..·ᵒ⌒°⌒·⌒°..

"Count the rings around my shell
If they're even, I'm not well.
If they're odd, I'll soon be hot
and steaming in your chowder pot."

Ralph Waldo Emerson
1803-1882

·°ᵒ⌒·:·⌒ᵒ°·

Count every ring!

Jackson Pollack Cake

Let your creative instincts go wild when you decorate this wonderful cake. Shake off your inhibitions and make your kitchen your studio.

Arrange the
frosting pallette.

Begin: Turn your
hand-mixer
on high

The masterpiece!

The authors of <u>Cooking</u> <u>for</u> <u>Nitwits</u> gratefully
acknowledge the generous support of the
following individuals and merchants.

Karen Juvonen
Ann & Charles Olcott
Phyllis Fogelman
Michael & Ruth Guden
Rick & Francis Hegenberger
Andy & Teddy Schwartz
Rainer Fishbach
Barbara O'Brien
Louise Cecil
Jan Anestis

Carol Ferguson
Martha Grimm
Burt Beekhuizen
Susan & Glenn Paulson
Marcella Winchell
Joanna Farber
Susan Rotando
Sherri Simerman
Ann Taylor
Deb Clark

The Kitchen Emporium, Briarcliff Manor, New York
The Cat's Meow, Westport, Connecticut
Harper's Furs, Fairfield, Connecticut
The Complete Kitchen, Wilton, Connecticut
Parc Monceau, Westport, Connecticut
Clementine's, Westport, Connecticut
New Pond Farm, Redding, Connecticut
Gallery of Linens, Westport, Connecticut